NICKELODEON

SpongeBob SquarePants™

KRUSTY KRAB ADVENTURES

Contributing Editor - Paul Morrissey
Graphic Design and Lettering - Dave Snow
Cover Layout - Raymond Makowski
Production Specialist and Additional Layout - Anna Kernbaum

Editor - Elizabeth Hurchalla
Managing Editor - Jill Freshney
Production Coordinator - Antonio DePietro
Production Manager - Jennifer Miller
Art Director - Matt Alford
Editorial Director - Jeremy Ross
VP of Production - Ron Klamert
President & C.O.O. - John Parker
Publisher & C.E.O. - Stuart Levy

Email: editor@TOKYOPOP.com
Come visit us online at www.TOKYOPOP.com

A TOKYOPOP® Cine-Manga™
TOKYOPOP® is an imprint of Mixx Entertainment, Inc.
5900 Wilshire Blvd., Suite 2000, Los Angeles, CA 90036

ISBN: 1-59182-398-6
First TOKYOPOP® printing: June 2003

10 9 8 7 6 5 4 3 2 1

Printed in Canada

NICKELODEON

SpongeBob SquarePants™

Created by Stephen Hillenburg

KRUSTY KRAB ADVENTURES

LOS ANGELES • TOKYO • LONDON

SPONGEBOB SQUAREPANTS: An optimistic and friendly sea sponge who lives in a pineapple with his snail, Gary, and works as a fry cook at The Krusty Krab. He loves his job and is always looking on the bright side of everything.

SQUIDWARD TENTACLES: A squid who works as the cashier at The Krusty Krab. Unlike SpongeBob, Squidward tends to be negative about everything. Secretly, he craves the limelight.

MR. KRABS: A crab who owns and runs The Krusty Krab. Mr. Krabs loves money and will do anything to avoid losing it. Mr. Krabs also adores his daughter, Pearl.

GARY: SpongeBob's pet snail. Meows like a cat.

PLANKTON: A plankton who constantly sneaks into The Krusty Krab attempting to get his hands on a Fa[illegible] Krabby Patty. Despite his size, Pl[illegible] be a big threat to Mr. K[illegible]

KRUSTY KRAB ADVENTURES

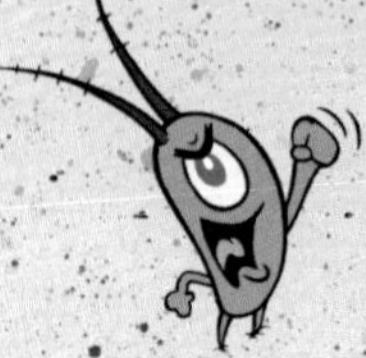

SpongeBob
SquarePants
TM
The Algae's
Always
Greener
by Aaron Springer, C.H. Greenblatt
and Merriwether Williams

THE KRUSTY KRAB
BOINK!
GALLEY GRUB
PARDON ME, YOUNG LADY!
OH! WHAT A FOX!
CONDIMENT ISLAND
WHIRRR

AHA!
HA
HA HAAA!
OOH HOO.
YOU'RE ALL
MINE, YOU SWEET
KRABBY PATTY.
OOH HOO. OOH HA
HA HA HA HA HA!
INITIATING
LAUNCH SEQUENCE!
KRABBY PATTY,
HERE I COME!!
EH... EH...
I HOPE I DON'T
MISS AGAIN.
ALERT!
ALERT!
SPLOOSH!
ZIP!
BUCKLE!

REUNITED! AND IT'S GONNA FEEL SO GOOD!!
AAAAAAAAAHHHHHH!
DER
ERE
WHIIZZZZZ
OOH, OOH, SWEET WAMPUM. HUH! WHAZZAT? ANOTHER ONE OF THOSE DRIVE-BY THINGS!
SQUIDWARD, WHERE ARE YOU? SHIELD ME WITH YOUR FOREHEAD!
SO! IT WAS JUST ANOTHER FAILED KRABBY PATTY THEFT ATTEMPT BY MY ARCH COMPETITOR, PLANKTON! FOR A SECOND THERE, I MISTOOK YOU FOR A THREAT!
BUT YOU'RE JUST A DIRTY LITTLE MAN!

FLINK!
SO LONG, SHRIMP!
CURSE YOU, MR. KRABS!!!!
WOOSH!
SO, TYPICAL DAY OF FAILURE, I SEE, HUH, DARLING?
SIGH!
OH, CAN IT, COMPUTER WIFE. CAN'T YOU SEE I'M EXHAUSTED? WHY DON'T YOU GO MAKE YOURSELF USEFUL AND SYNTHESIZE ME UP SOME GRUB?
YES, YOUR MAJESTY.
ZAP!

WHAT DO WE GOT HERE?
OH GOODY. HOLOGRAPHIC MEATLOAF AGAIN!
SMASH!
WHEN AM I GONNA GET SOME REAL FOOD! MISTER KRABS GETS TO EAT REAL FOOD. JUST LOOK AT HIS DAUGHTER... SHE'S AS BIG AS A WHALE!
I WISH I COULD BE SUCCESSFUL LIKE MR. KRABS. I WISH I COULD SOMEHOW JUST SWITCH LIVES WITH HIM, JUST TO KNOW WHAT IT'S LIKE.
THEN WHY DON'T YOU JUST USE THAT "SWITCH-LIVES-JUST-TO-KNOW-WHAT-IT'S-LIKE-O-MOGRIFIER" THING YOU BUILT LAST TUESDAY?
WHAT A BRILLIANT IDEA! YOUR PARENTS MUST HAVE BEEN, LIKE, PART COMPUTER OR SOMETHING.
NOW, LET'S SEE HERE... NO...
NO...
NO...

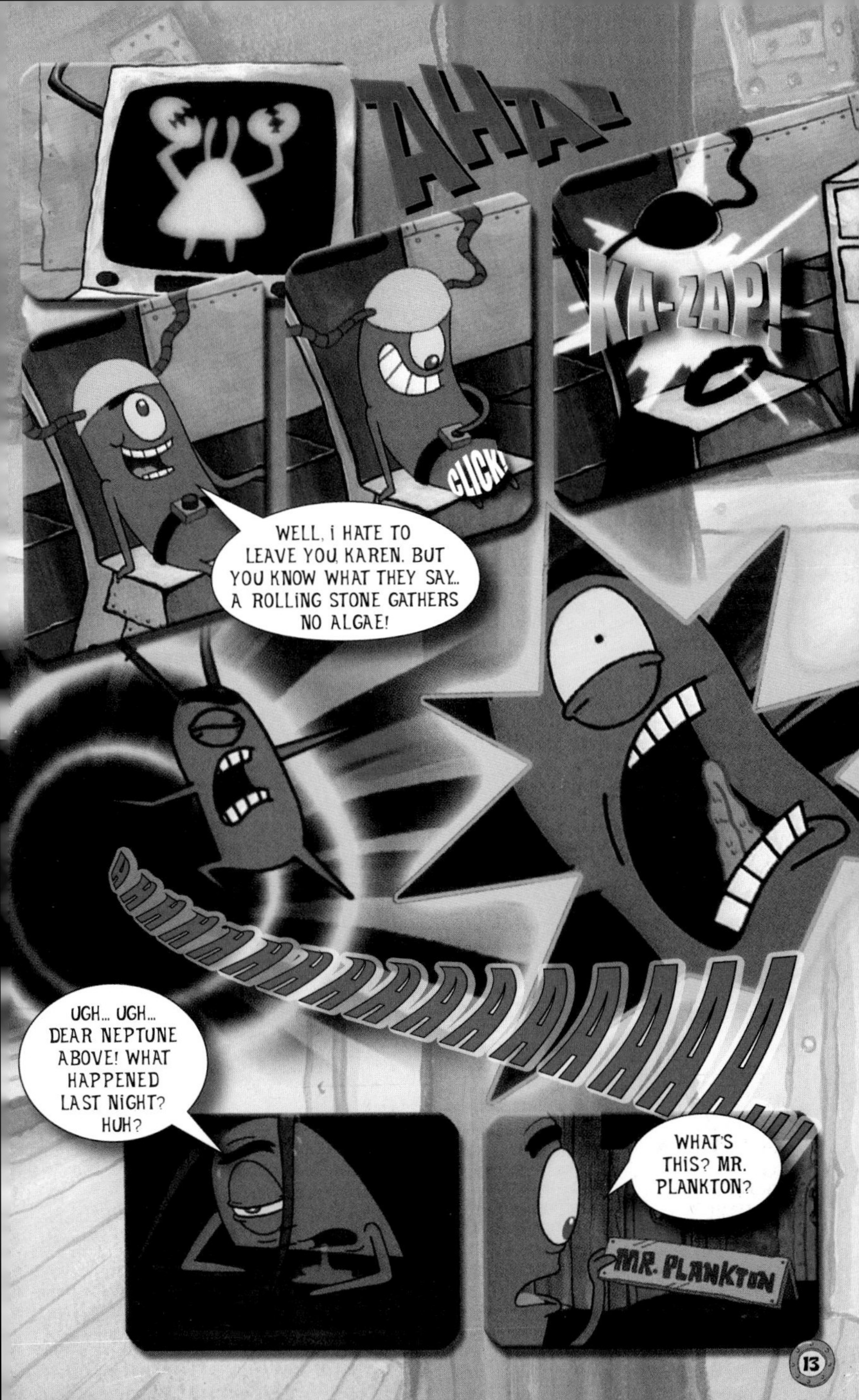
AHA!
CLICK!
KA-ZAP!
WELL, i HATE TO LEAVE YOU, KAREN. BUT YOU KNOW WHAT THEY SAY... A ROLLING STONE GATHERS NO ALGAE!
AAAAAAAAAAAAAAAAAAAAA...
UGH... UGH... DEAR NEPTUNE ABOVE! WHAT HAPPENED LAST NiGHT? HUH?
WHAT'S THiS? MR. PLANKTON?
MR. PLANKTON

WHO THE DAVEY?
EH? I'M IN THE KRUSTY KRAB.
THEN THAT MEANS THE LIFE SWITCHER WAS A SUCCESS!
THE KRUSTY KRAB IS MINE!
ORDER UP!
TWO DELUXE KRABBY PATTIES!
THERE YOU ARE, SIR! TWO DELUXE...
AT LAST!

AHOY THERE, MR. PLANKTON!
ER, UM, HEY THERE, UH, SPONGEBOB! UH, SPONGEBOB?
YES, SIR!
I'M GONNA NEED TO TAKE ONE OF THESE PATTIES BACK TO MY OFFICE FOR, UM, BUN INSPECTION!
I'M AFRAID YOU CAN'T DO THAT, MR. PLANKTON!
WH- WHY NOT?
BECAUSE THAT PATTY IS FOR THE CUSTOMER, SIR!
THE CUSTOMER? I'LL BOIL THE CUSTOMER IN HOT OIL AND I'LL RIP OUT HIS...
ENTER
ENTER

I MEAN, UH, YES! OF COURSE! FOR THE LOVELY CUSTOMER!
BUT YOU CAN TAKE THESE PATTIES, SIR! I MADE THEM ON THE OFF CHANCE YOU DECIDED TO INSTIGATE SOME BUN INSPECTION TODAY, MR. PLANKTON, SIR!
UH...YES, UH, VERY NICE, UM... THANKS!
WOOSH!
AHHH!
ALL MINE! IT'S FINALLY ALL MINE... THE PATTIES, THE WEALTH, THE NOTORIETY! THE...
SPONGEBOB? WHAT DO YOU WANT?
WELL, IT'S JUST THAT IT'S TUESDAY AGAIN, SIR, AND I WAS WONDERING IF I COULD HAVE MY, UMMM...MM...WEEKLY PERFORMANCE REVIEW?!

REVIEW?
OH YES, PLEASE, SIR, PLEASE!!
EECH! YOU'RE DOING FINE. NOW LEAVE ME TO MY WORK.
BUT, SIR...!
I THOUGHT I SENT YOU AWAY, CRETIN!
BUT, SIR, THERE'S GOT TO BE SOMETHING I NEED TO IMPROVE ON...ANYTHING!
ALL RIGHT! THE SAUCE! I DUNNO, YOU'RE USING TOO MUCH SAUCE, OKAY? REVIEW'S OVER!
UH... UH... UH... UH... UH... UH... UH...

UH... UH... UH... UH... UH...
WHATSA MATTER WITH YOU? ALL I SAID WAS "A LITTLE TOO MUCH SAUCE." IT'S NO BIG DEAL! REALLY!
WHAT DO YOU WANT FROM ME? A PROMOTION?
A PRO- A PROM- A PROMOTION?!
UH, SURE, KID... YOU'RE, UH... YOU'RE ON REGISTER NOW.
REGISTER!!!!!
GLAD THAT'S OVER!
SMMOOCH!

SPONGEBOB, DO YOU REMEMBER THAT LITTLE TALK WE HAD ABOUT "PERSONAL SPACE"?
IT'S OKAY, SQUIDWARD! I'M OFFICIAL! LOOK!
CO-CASHIER
CO-CASHIER?
YOU CAN'T DO THIS TO ME, MR. PLANKTON! IF YOU THINK I'M GOING TO STAND OUT THERE ALL DAY LISTENING TO...
YABBER YABBER YABBER
...THEN YOU MUST HAVE CORAL WEDGED IN YOUR FRONTAL LOBE!
YABBER YABBER YABBER YABBER YABBER YABBER YABBER YABBER YABBER YABBER
SO WHAT DO YOU WANT ME TO DO ABOUT IT?
I'D LIKE MY VIEW TO BE A LITTLE LESS YELLOW, IF YOU KNOW WHAT I MEAN.

HEY, SQUIDWARD! I CAN SEE YOU THROUGH THIS LITTLE WINDOW!
GROAN
NOW, NO MORE INTRUSIONS! I'D LIKE TO BEGIN WRITING THE MEMOIRS OF MY SUCCESS STORY, SO EVERYONE JUST STAY THE—
DADDY DADDY DADDY DADDY!
BAM!
BAM!
BAM!
OOF
OOF
OOF
SPLAT!
OOF! JUST TELL DADDY WHAT YOU WANT! ARF! HE'S VERY BUSY!! URF!
COULD I PLEASE HAVE A...UM... AN ADVANCE ON MY ALLOWANCE?
IF IT'LL GET YOU OUT OF MY ANTENNAE... GO CRAZY.

ONE DOLLAR? YOU HATE ME!

GUSH!
GUSH!
GUSH!

GLUGGHHH... GLUGGHHHH!!

YOU...

ME?

YOU THINK THIS IS FUNNY?

WHAT? IT'S JUST AN ORDINARY KRABBY—
OH MY GOODNESS!!

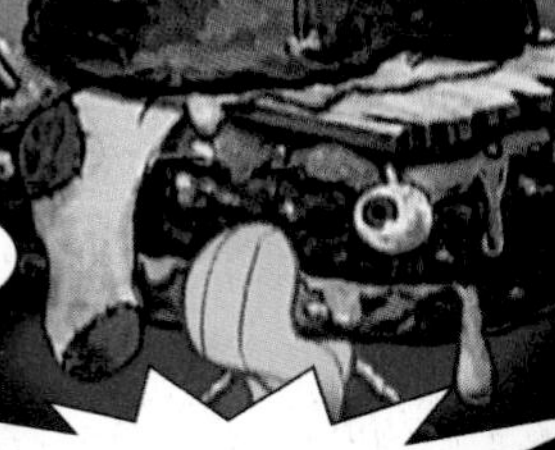
SQUIDWARD!

A CUSTOMER ORDERED A MEDIUM SODA AND I GAVE HIM A LARGE. I GAVE HIM A LARGE!!!
WHAT NOW?
I'VE SOILED THE GOOD KRUSTY KRAB NAME!
I COMMAND YOU TO STOP THAT! STOP THAT AND RETURN TO YOUR POST.
SOILED IT! SOILED IT! SOILED IT! SOILED IT! SOILED IT! SOILED IT! SOILED IT! SOILED IT! SOILED IT!
OKAY, DADDY! I'VE DECIDED I'M GONNA RUN AWAY! RUN AWAY AND FIND A NEW DADDY!
MAKE IT STOP!
SILENCE
WAAAAAA!
SOILED IT! SOILED IT! SOILED IT!
WHAT? DID I SAY THE SECRET WORD?

NO, SIR... HE'S BACK.
WHO'S BACK? WHAT?
WHAT WAS THAT?
WOOSH!
WOOOOP! WOOOOP!
MAN YOUR STATIONS! RED ALERT! RED ALERT! TAKE COVER!!
TAKE COVER FROM WHAT?!
AAAAAAHHH!

HE'S AROUND HERE SOMEWHERE!
WOOSH!
THERE HE GOES!
WHAT... WHO... WHERE?! SOMEBODY TELL ME.
SOME SAY HE CRAWLED OUT FROM THE LOWEST TRENCH IN THE OCEAN.
HE'S THE MOST HATED CREATURE IN BIKINI BOTTOM.
HE'S THE SALTIEST OF ALL THE SEA DOGS.
AND HE'S FINALLY GOT A KRABBY PATTY!! AR AR AR AR!

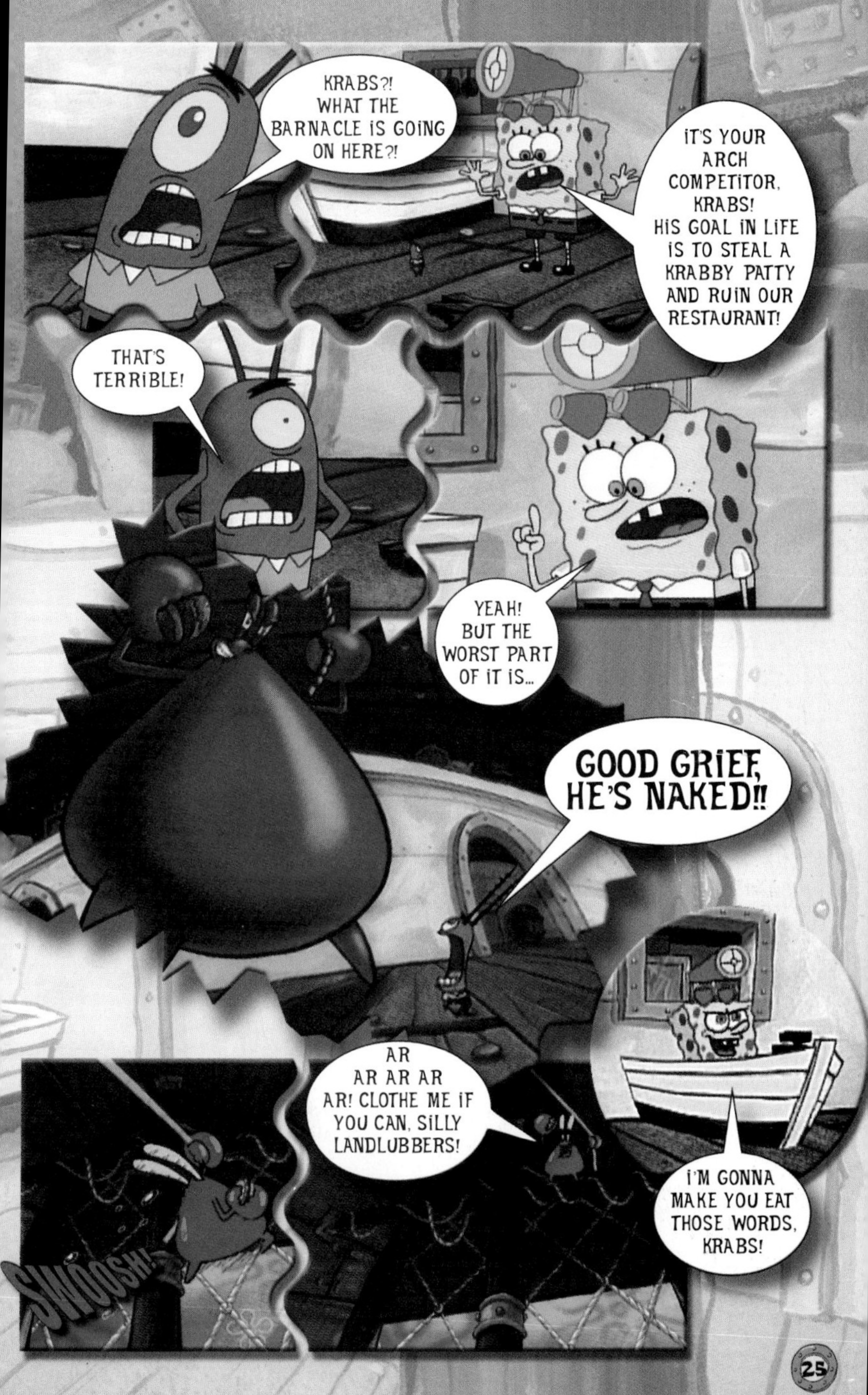
KRABS?! WHAT THE BARNACLE IS GOING ON HERE?!
IT'S YOUR ARCH COMPETITOR, KRABS! HIS GOAL IN LIFE IS TO STEAL A KRABBY PATTY AND RUIN OUR RESTAURANT!
THAT'S TERRIBLE!
YEAH! BUT THE WORST PART OF IT IS...
GOOD GRIEF, HE'S NAKED!!
AR AR AR AR AR! CLOTHE ME IF YOU CAN, SILLY LANDLUBBERS!
I'M GONNA MAKE YOU EAT THOSE WORDS, KRABS!
SWOOSH!

NO SHIRT...
NO SHOES...
NO SERVICE!
POW!
AHAHAHA
AR
AR
AR
AR!
HUH?
AW! YA
GOT ME!
WELL...
AT LEAST IT'S
UNDERWIRE. HERE'S
YOUR STINKIN'
PATTY!
KNICK-
KNACK, THE
PATTY'S BACK!!
YOU DID IT, MR.
PLANKTON!
VICTORY
SCREECH!
YAAAAAALP!

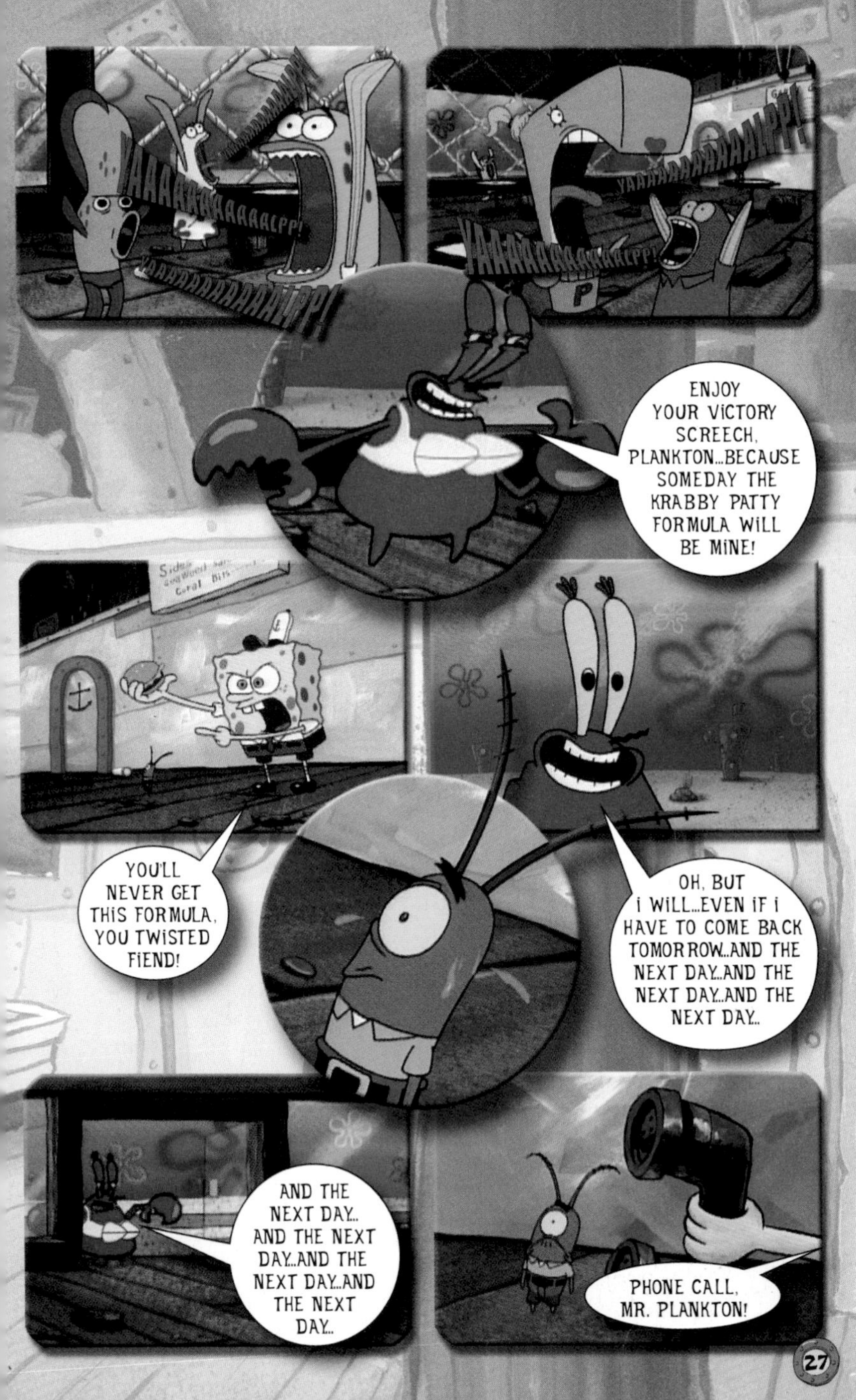
YAAAAAAAAAAAALPP!
YAAAAAAAAAAAALPP!
YAAAAAAAAAAAALPP!
YAAAAAAAAAAAALPP!
YAAAAAAAAAAAALPP!
ENJOY YOUR VICTORY SCREECH, PLANKTON...BECAUSE SOMEDAY THE KRABBY PATTY FORMULA WILL BE MINE!
YOU'LL NEVER GET THIS FORMULA, YOU TWISTED FIEND!
OH, BUT I WILL...EVEN IF I HAVE TO COME BACK TOMORROW...AND THE NEXT DAY...AND THE NEXT DAY...AND THE NEXT DAY...
AND THE NEXT DAY... AND THE NEXT DAY...AND THE NEXT DAY...AND THE NEXT DAY...
PHONE CALL, MR. PLANKTON!

AND THE NEXT DAY...
AND THE NEXT DAY...
AND THE NEXT DAY...
AND THE...
AAAAAAAAA!
RIP!
SHRED!
TEAR!
IT'S NOT WORTH IT! IT'S JUST NOT WORTH IT!
GOODBYE, EVERYONE! I'LL REMEMBER YOU ALL IN THERAPY.
KA-ZAP!
HOLOGRAPHIC MEATLOAF? MY FAVORITE!!
CHUM BUCKET
THE END

SpongeBob SquarePants™

Culture Shock

by Paul Tibbit, Mark O'Hare and Mr. Lawrence

THE KRUSTY KRAB
FREE SALAD BAR FREE
AHHHH...
HMMM...
FREE!
NO CHARGE
FREE!
I JUST DON'T GET IT. IF A FREE SALAD BAR DOESN'T BRING IN CUSTOMERS...WHAT WILLLLLLLLL?!?!
DA DEE DUM, DA DEE DOO...
FREE SALAD BAR FREE
SQUIDWARD!!! THERE'S GONNA BE SOME CHANGES AROUND HERE.

GASP!
A CUSTOMER!
FREE!
WELCOME TO THE KRUSTY KRAB!
SPONGEBOB?! CATER TO HIS EVERY WHIM. AND DON'T SCREW THIS ONE UP!
AYE-AYE, SIR!

WELCOME ABOARD, SIR! HERE AT THE KRUSTY KRAB, YOU ARE THE CAPTAIN...AND I, A MERE CABIN BOY.
YOU JUST SAY THE WORD...AND I'LL THROW MYSELF IN THE BRIG! MAY I TAKE YOUR ORDER?
ALL I WANTED WAS CHANGE FOR THE PAY PHONE.
AYE-AYE, SIR!!
WOOSH!
MON SEWERS... CHANGE!
THANKS! HEH HEH. HERE YA GO.

YAH!!
SLAM!
AS YOU MAY HAVE NOTICED, PROFITS ARE WAY DOWN THIS MONTH.
WE NEED A GIMMICK TO BRING IN CUSTOMERS. DO YOU LUBBERS HAVE ANY IDEAS?
I'VE GOT ONE!

A FREE PAIR OF SOCKS WITH EVERY PURCHASE!
ahem!
DANCE NOW!
OR MAYBE DOUBLE PATTY MIDNIGHT MADNESS!
OOH! OOH! OOH! OOH! OOH! OOH! I KNOW I KNOW I KNOW! HOW ABOUT A MOUTHFUL OF CLAMS DAY! EVERYONE WHO SHOWS UP WITH A MOUTHFUL OF CLAMS...
...GETH A FWEE DWINK! HUH? HUH?
WELL...I WAS THINKIN' MORE ALONG THE LINES OF LIVE ENTERTAINMENT.
THAT'S IT! A FLOOR SHOW! NO! WAIT! A TALENT SHOW!

WITH YOUR HOST...ME! THIS IS THE MOMENT I'VE— I MEAN, WE'VE BEEN DREAMING OF!
THINK OF IT, MR. KRABS! YOU WILL BE RESPONSIBLE FOR BRINGING CULTURE TO THIS CULTURAL WASTELAND WE CALL BIKINI BOTTOM! AND NOT TO MENTION THE MONEY.
THE MONEY?!
AND I CAN SEE IT NOW! YOUR DAUGHTER PEARL! HER NAME UP IN LIGHTS.
LITTLE PEARLIE! A STAR?!
HOPPIN' CLAMS! A TALENT SHOW. I'M TALENTED. I BETTER CALL THE FOLKS!
SQUIDWARD, YOU'VE GOT A DEAL. MAKE MY LITTLE GIRL A STAR!

HEY, SQUIDWARD! WHAT TIME AM I GOING ON?
GOING ON WHAT?
THE SHOW! WHEN AM I GOING ON THE SHOW? I HAVE A GREAT ACT!
WHAT TALENT COULD YOU POSSIBLY POSSESS?
DRIP

NO ONE... NOT EVEN YOUR PARENTS...WOULD WANT TO SEE THAT.

WHAT THE PEOPLE WANT IS CULTURE, NOT DANCING BUBBLES!

I CAN HARDLY WAIT.

WOW! A FULL HOUSE! THERE'S MOM 'N' DAD. THEY ARE GONNA BE SO PROUD!
I BETTER GET READY!
HELLOOOOO. I'M MR. KRABS, AND I LIKE MONEY!
ALL RIGHT. LISTEN UP, PEOPLE! LISTEN UP! GATHER 'ROUND, EVERYONE! CHOP-CHOP! YOU MAY BE THINKING THIS IS YOUR ONE SHOT AT THE BIGTIME. WELL, IT'S NOT.
IT'S MINE.
SHLOOP!
HEY, SQUID! HOW ABOUT THIS FOR THE SHOW! THE AMAZING MR. ABSORBENCY!
MISTER ABSORBENCY
M

GRUNT!
TA-DA!
NO ONE
iS GONNA
WANT TO SEE
YOU ENGORGE
YOURSELF.
PLEASE,
SQUiDWARD! LET
ME BE iN THE SHOW!
i'LL DO ANYTHiNG!
ANYTHiNG!!
ANYTHiNG!!
SO YOU
REALLY WANT TO
BE iN THE SHOW?
OH, YES!
OKAY. YOU
GET TO MOP UP
AFTERWARD! NOW
WiLL YOU STOP
BUGGiNG ME?
SO THiS
iS WHAT iT FEELS
LiKE...THE
BiGTiME.

WITH THIS MOP I SHAPE MY DESTINY!
AHEM. GOOD EVENING AND WELCOME TO THE FIRST ANNUAL SQUIDWARD TENTACLES TALENT SHOW. SPONSORED BY THE KRUSTY KRAB, HOME OF THE KRABBY PATTY...
...BECAUSE NO ONE ELSE WOULD GIVE IT A HOME.
HA - HA - HA - HA - BWAA - HA - HA - HA. HA - AHH - HA - HA - HA - HA - HA - HA - HA - HA...
THANK YOU! OUR NEXT ACT IS LIVING PROOF THAT NEPOTISM IS ALIVE AND WELL.
PUT YOUR FINS TOGETHER FOR... PEARL.

GASP!
HOORAY! MY LITTLE GIRL IS FINALLY A STAR!
GIMME A K-R-U!
BOOM!
AIGHHHHHH!
GIMME A S-T-Y!
BOOM!
AIGHHHHHH!
KRUSTY KRAB!
AIGHHHHHH!
BOOM!

KRUSTY KRAB!

AIGHHHHHH!

OOF!

BOOM!

KRUSTY KRAB!

OOHHH OOHH...

EEE!!

AIGHHHHHH!

BOOM!

OW!

NOW THAT'S WHAT I CALL TALENT!

THANK YOU!

HEY, SQUIDWARD! LISTEN, WHAT DO YOU THINK? WHEN I MOP, SHOULD I GO FORWARD AND BACK?

NO, NO, WAIT! SIDE TO SIDE!

WOOSH!
AND NOW, POETRY BY GARY.
MEOW, MEOW, MEOW, MEOW.
AH...HE HAS SUCH A WAY WITH WORDS.
COME ON... COME ON, GINSBERG... IF HE DOESN'T HURRY IT UP, WE'RE NOT GONNA HAVE ENOUGH TIME FOR THE BEST ACT... **ME.**
SQUIDWARD? SHOULD I USE... MR. CLEANSER? OR DR. CLEAN?
YES.
I...THE AMAZING PLANKTON... WITH THE USE OF PRESTIDIGITATION...
THE AMAZING PLANKTON !!!

...WILL MAKE A KRABBY PATTY DISAPPEAR BEFORE YOUR VERY EYE!
FIRST, I'LL NEED A VOLUNTEER FROM THE AUDIENCE.
HUH?
SNEAK SNEAK SNEAK
NICE TRY! YOUR ACT'S OVER, BUG.
SWIPE!
YOU MAY WIN THIS TIME!
CHEE-YOK KA-ZING!

KA-BOOM!!
WELL, THIS STINKS!
SQUIDWARD! THIS SHOW IS A DISASTER! YOU'RE RUININ' ME!
BOOOO!
BOOOO!
HISS!
NOW... NOW...DON'T YOU WORRY, MR. KRABS. I'VE SAVED THE BEST FOR LAST. YOU'LL SEE.
FOR YOUR SAKE, I HOPE YOU'RE RIGHT!
AND NOW...LADIES AND GENTLEMEN...THE MOMENT YOU'VE ALL BEEN WAITING FOR... WE'VE SAVED THE BEST FOR LAST. PUT YOUR HANDS TOGETHER FOR...THE INCOMPARABLE SQUIDWARD!
TA-DA!

WHAT TH—?!
SALAD BAR
BOOOO!
HISS!
BOOOO!
SPLAT!
I'M LOSIN' MONEY ON THIS DEAL!

iT'S WORTH EVERY PENNY!
MORE TOMATOES, PLEASE.
BOOOO!
HISS!
YOU BOTTOM FEEDERS! YOU DON'T EVEN KNOW TALENT!
NO TALENT! NO TALENT! NO TALENT!
HEY, SQUiDWARD, CAN i GO ON NOW?!
YEAH! SHOW'S OVER!!
BOOOO!
BOOOO!
BOOOO!
BOOOO!
BOOOO!
BOOOO!

YEAH!
YEAH!
ALL RIGHT!
CLAP
CLAP
CLAP
CLAP

HURRAHHHHH!
CLAP
CLAP
CLAP
THEY WANT AN ENCORE!
CLAP

HURRAHHHHH!
CLAP
CLAP
HURRAHHHHH!
STAND ASIDE, SPONGEBOB.
CLAP

SILENCE
STOMP
STOMP
STOMP

YEAAAAAAAAHH!

YEAH!
WOO-HOO!

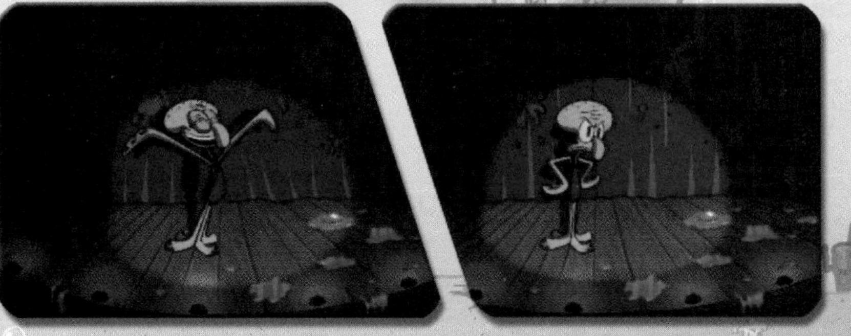

YEAAAAAAAAHH!

YEAAAAAAAAHH!

HURRAHHHHH!

YEAAAAAHH
SPLAT!
YEAAAAAAAAAAHH!
MY SON'S A STAR!
WHO EVER KNEW HE HAD SUCH TALENT?!
YEAH!
HURRAHHHHH!
ENCORE!
YOU DID IT, SQUIDWARD! WHAT A GREAT SHOW!
I'LL BE NEEDIN' ANOTHER WHEELBARROW FOR NEXT WEEK'S SHOW!
THE END

Pizza Delivery

by Sherm Cohen, Aaron Springer and Peter Burns

THE KRUSTY KRAB
SCRUB
SCRUB
RING
RING
HURRY UP WITH THOSE CHAIRS, SPONGEBOB. IT'S AFTER CLOSING AND I'D LIKE TO GO HOME!
I GOT IT! I GOT IT! COMING!
HELLO? OH, SORRY, SIR, WE'RE CLOSED...
AHOY THERE! KRUSTY KRAB! HOW CAN I HELP YOU? PIZZA? OF COURSE WE HAVE PIZZA!
SWIPE
UH, MR. KRABS?

OUR DELIVERY SQUID WILL BRING IT RIGHT OVER!
MR. KRABS, WE DON'T SERVE PIZZA. WE DON'T DELIVER.
SNIP!
ROLL!
CUT!
WE DON'T DELIVER, BUT YOU DO!
CAN'T YOU JUST GET SPONGEBOB TO DO IT?
GREAT IDEA! TAKE HIM WITH YA!

FRONT END—CHECK! ANTENNA—CHECK! BUMPER—CHECK!
BUMPER STICKER—CHECK!
I Brake FoR Sea Urchins
TIRE PRESSURE—
WHOOO!
SHOOOOOOOP!
CHECK! VEHICLE INSPECTION COMPLETE!
WE'RE REALLY MAKING HISTORY HERE, SQUIDWARD. DO YOU REALIZE THAT?! THAT LUCKY CUSTOMER IS GONNA GET THE FIRST KRABBY PATTY PIZZA EVER.

GOOD— THEN YOU DRIVE.
I CAN'T. I'M STILL IN BOATING SCHOOL.
COME ON, SPONGEBOB! IT'S JUST AROUND THE CORNER!
WELL, YEAH, BUT...
WELL, OKAY. WAIT. DON'T TELL ME.
JUST DO WHAT YOU DO IN SCHOOL!
BACK IT UP! SHIFT INTO REVERSE, SPONGEBOB!
REVERSE— OH YEAH, REVERSE.

BACK IT UP!

BAAAAAACKING UUUUUUUUUPP!!!

GIVE ME THE WHEEL, SPONGEBOB! GIVE ME THE WHEEL!!

BACKING UP!

BACKING UP!

AAAAAAAAAA!

BACKING UP... BACKING UP... BACKING UP... BACKING UP...

WELL, YOU BACKED UP!

AND YOU KNOW WHAT? I THINK WE'RE OUT OF GAS!

SCREECH!

AND YOU KNOW WHAT ELSE? WE'RE IN THE MIDDLE OF NOWHERE!
AND YOU KNOW WHAT ELSE? I THINK THE PIZZA'S GETTING COLD.
AND THE PIZZA'S COLD! OOH! THE PIZZA'S COLD! NOT THE PIZZA!
BAM!
WHIR!
CREAK!
Fuel
SPUTTER!
OH, HOW COULD IT GET ANY WORSE?!
SPUTTER!
SPUTTER!
WELL, WE CAN STILL DELIVER IT ON FOOT.

THE KRUSTY KRAB PIZZA IS THE PIZZA FOR YOU AND ME! THE KRUSTY KRAB PIZZA IS THE PIZZA...
OW! OW OW! MY FEET ARE KILLING ME!
WHOA!
OOF! SPONGEBOB, WHAT ARE YOU DOING?!
IT'S AN OLD PIONEER TRICK. I SAW IT IN A MOVIE ONCE!
SPONGEBOB! THIS IS NO TIME FOR...
SSHHHH! IT'S WORKING!
TRUCK! SIXTEEN WHEELS! NOW I CAN SHOW YOU HOW THE PIONEERS HITCHHIKED!
PIZZA

EEEYEEEYEEEYEEE-
YEEEEYEEEEYEEEE!!!
LOUSY
BREAKDANCERS!
HE'S
STOPPiNG! HE'S
STOPPiNG!
HONK!
HONK!
SMASH!
SQUISH!
ZOOM!

THE KRUSTY KRAB PIZZA...IS THE PIZZA...FOR YOU AND ME! THE KRUSTY KRAB PIZZA... IS THE PIZZA...FREE DELIVERY! THE KRUSTY KRAB PIZZA...IS THE PIZZA...VERY TASTY!
WOOSH!
WOOOP!!!
SWOOSH!
GUST!
AAAAAAAAA!
WILL YOU LET GO OF THAT STUPID PIZZA ALREADY?
GUST!
I CAN'T! IT'S FOR THE CUSTOMER!
WHO CARES ABOUT THE CUSTOMER?!
I DO!
GUST!
SWOOSH!

WELL, I DON'T!
HUH? SQUIDWARD!
SWOOSH!
LET GO OF THAT PIZZA!
NO!
GUST!
BOOF!
OUCH! SPONGEBOB! LET GO OF THE PIZZA!
NO! IT'S FOR THE CUSTOMER!
SPONGE-BOB! LET GO OF THE PIZZA!
GUST!
SWOOSH!
NO!
WOOSH!

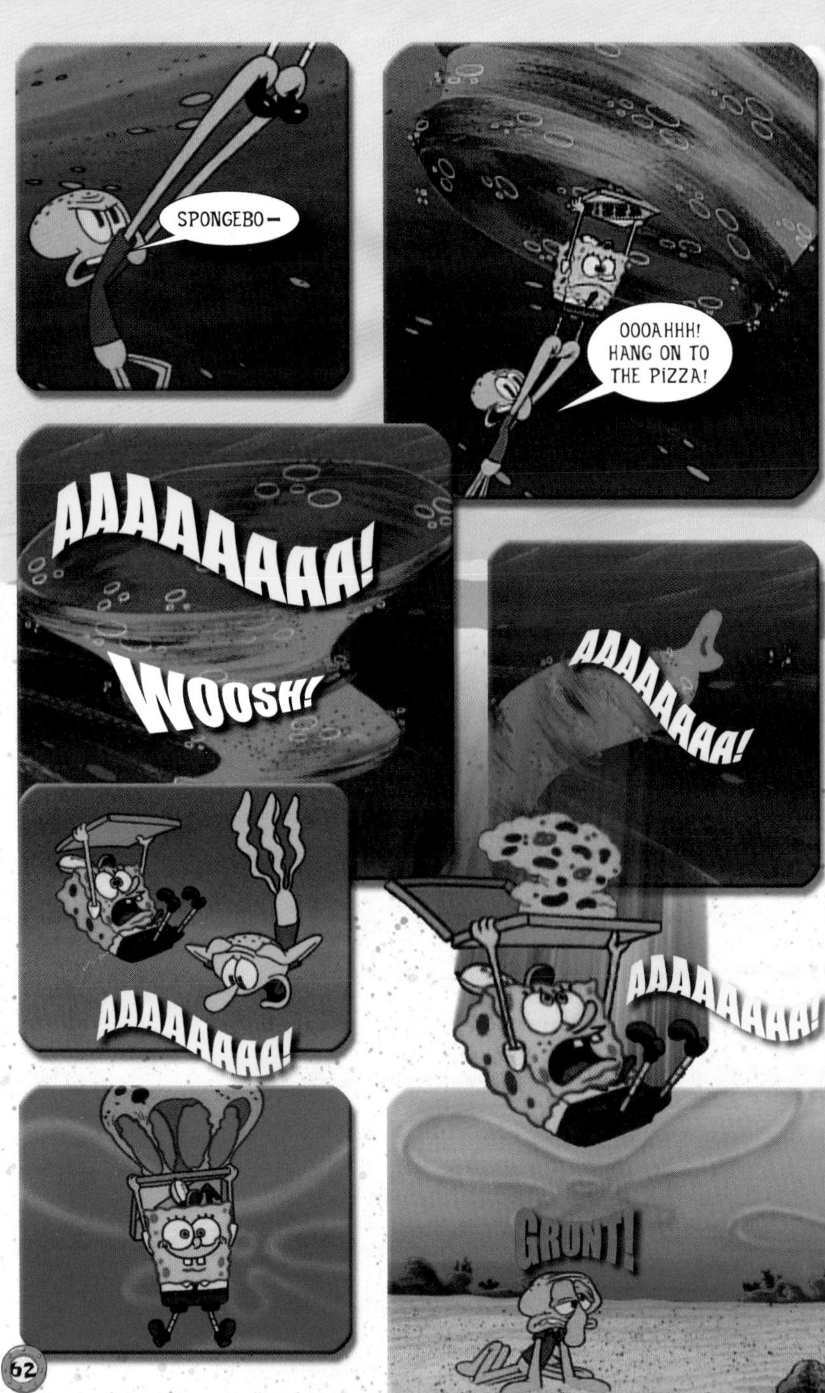
SPONGEBO—
OOOAHHH! HANG ON TO THE PIZZA!
AAAAAAAAA!
WOOSH!
AAAAAAAAA!
AAAAAAAAA!
AAAAAAAAA!
GRUNT!

HEY... WH- WHERE-WHERE'S THE ROAD?
WE'RE DOOMED!
HOW ARE WE GONNA GET HOME? WHICH WAY DO WE GO? WHAT ARE WE GONNA DO? THERE'S NO ROAD HERE.
I THINK TOWN'S THIS WAY.
DON'T TELL ME, "JETHRO"... THE PIONEERS?

THAT'S RIGHT! MOSS ALWAYS POINTS TO CIVILIZATION.
THAT WAY, THAT WAY THERE. SO LET ME GET THIS STRAIGHT, YOU THINK THAT WE SHOULD GO THAT WAY?
YEP.
WELL, I'M GOING THIS WAY.
WAIT! I DON'T THINK...
TRUST ME—I KNOW WHERE I'M GOING!
IN THE OPPOSITE DIRECTION:
CIVILIZATION

THE KRUSTY KRAB PIZZA! IS THE PIZZA! AB-SO-LOO-TIV-E-LEE! DA DOO DOO BA DA DA DOOO BOO DOO TOO TOO TEE TEE!

KRUSTY KRAB PIZZA IS THE PIZZA—KRAAAAAAYAAYAAAYAYAYAA—AAAAAYAYAYAYAYAAAB BA DA DOO...FOR YOU AND ME.

KRUSTY KRAB PIZZA... PIZZA... KRAB... KRUST... KRAB... PIZZA... FOR... YOU... KRUST.. KRUSTY... KRU...

WHAM!

GOT TO EAT SOMETHING!

CRACK!
NO— MAYBE IT WASN'T CORAL... MAYBE IT WAS SAND... NO... MUD?
OR MAYBE...
GIMME THE PIZZA!
WAIT! I REMEMBER NOW—IT WAS CORAL!
GIVE IT TO ME!
NO! WE PROMISED. IT'S FOR THE CUSTOMER!
YOU'RE RIGHT. IT'S FOR THE CUSTOMER.

MAYBE WE'D BETTER CHECK ON IT... MAKE SURE IT'S OKAY.
WELL...
JUST A PEEK.
OKAY, IT'S FINE!
NO! I THINK I SAW SOMETHING!
OH, NOPE, I WAS WRONG. IT LOOKS OKAY.
IT SURE IS A FINE-LOOKING PIZZA.

WHAT'S THAT? IS THAT CHEESE? AND PEPPERONI...
YEAH...
OH, LOOKS GOOD, HUH?
WAIT A SECOND... I KNOW WHAT YOU'RE TRYING TO DO, SQUIDWARD. I'M NOT LETTING YOU EAT THE PIZZA!
GIMME THAT PIZZA!
I WANT THAT PIZZA! AND YOU'RE GONNA HAND IT OVER—ONE WAY OR ANOTHER!

SURE, WE'RE SAVED. NOW GIMME SOME PIZZA!
NO, REALLY, SQUID! WE'RE SAVED! WE'RE SAVED! WE'RE SAVED! SAVED!
THAT'S JUST A STUPID BOULDER!
IT'S NOT JUST A BOULDER! (SNIFF) IT'S A ROCK! IT'S A BIG—BEAUTIFUL—OLD—ROCK! THE PIONEERS USED TO RIDE THESE BABIES FOR MILES! AND IT'S IN GREAT SHAPE.
SPONGEBOB?!! WILL YOU FORGET THE STUPID PIONEERS?! HAVE YOU EVER NOTICED THAT THERE ARE NONE OF THEM LEFT?!! THAT'S BECAUSE THEY WERE LOUSY HITCHHIKERS, ATE CORAL AND TOOK DIRECTIONS FROM ALGAE!
AND NOW YOU'RE TELLIN' ME THEY THOUGHT THEY COULD DRIVE...
...ROCKS.
HOLD ON THERE, JETHRO!

I CAN'T WAIT TO SEE THE LOOK ON OUR CUSTOMER'S FACE!
DING-DONG
CONGRATULATIONS, SIR! YOUR KRABBY PATTY PIZZA IS HERE!
WOW! THANKS! I'VE BEEN DYIN' FOR ONE OF THESE. WHERE'S MY DRINK?
WHAT DRINK?
MY DRINK! MY DIET DR. KELP! DON'T TELL ME YOU FORGOT MY DRINK?!
BUT YOU DIDN'T ORDER ANY—

HOW'M I SUPPOSED TO EAT THIS PIZZA WITHOUT MY DRINK? DIDN'T YOU EVER ONCE THINK OF THE CUSTOMER?! YOU CALL YOURSELF A DELIVERY BOY?
WHAP
PIZZA
WELL, I AIN'T BUYIN'!
BUH-HUH-HUH!
SNIFF
BUH-HUH-HUH!
BAM!
BAM!
BAM!
ANOTHER ONE? LOOK, I TOLD YOUR LITTLE FRIEND I AIN'T PAYIN' FOR THAT!
WELL, THIS ONE'S ON THE HOUSE!
PIZZA
SMASH!

DID HE CHANGE HIS MIND?
SNIFF
HE SURE DID! ATE THE WHOLE THING IN ONE BITE.
NO DRINK?
NAH... NOW TAKE ME HOME.
ARE YOU KIDDING? WE HAVE JUST ENOUGH TIME TO MAKE IT BACK TO WORK!
WORK?
OH, MY ACHING TENTACLES!
THE END

SpongeBob SquarePants™

Pickles

by Steve Fonti, Chris Mitchell and Peter Burns

THE KRUSTY KRAB
HMMM... UH...I'LL HAVE...UH...
HMMM... MAYBE...I'LL HAVE...
GALLEY GRUB
KRABBY PATTY ... 2 00
KRUSTY COMBO 3 99
KRUSTY DELUXE... 3 00
Sides
SeaWeed Salad... 1 50
Coral Bits........ 1 95
ARE YOU PLANNING TO ORDER TODAY, SIR?
I'LL HAVE A KRABBY PATTY.
OH, HOW ORIGINAL.
AND WITH EXTRA ONIONS.
DARING TODAY, AREN'T WE?

ONE CRYING JOHNNY, UP!
WHATEVER! TWELVE KRABBY PATTIES ON WHEAT BUNS!
ONE DOZEN CRYING COWS ON THE FARM, UP!
IT'S BEEN A THRILL SERVING YOU.
LET ME GUESS, TINY, A SMALL SALAD?

I'LL TAKE A DOUBLE TRIPLE BOSSY DELUXE ON A RAFT, 4X4 ANIMAL STYLE, EXTRA SHINGLES WITH A SHIMMY AND A SQUEEZE, LIGHT AXLE GREASE, MAKE IT CRY, BURN IT AND LET IT SWIM.
WE SERVE FOOD HERE, SIR.
I GOT IT ALREADY, SQUIDWARD.
GASP! BUBBLEBASS.
SQUAREPANTS! I HEAR TALK YOU MAKE A MEAN KRABBY PATTY.
YEP...
I HEAR TALK YER KINDA PICKY.
YEP.

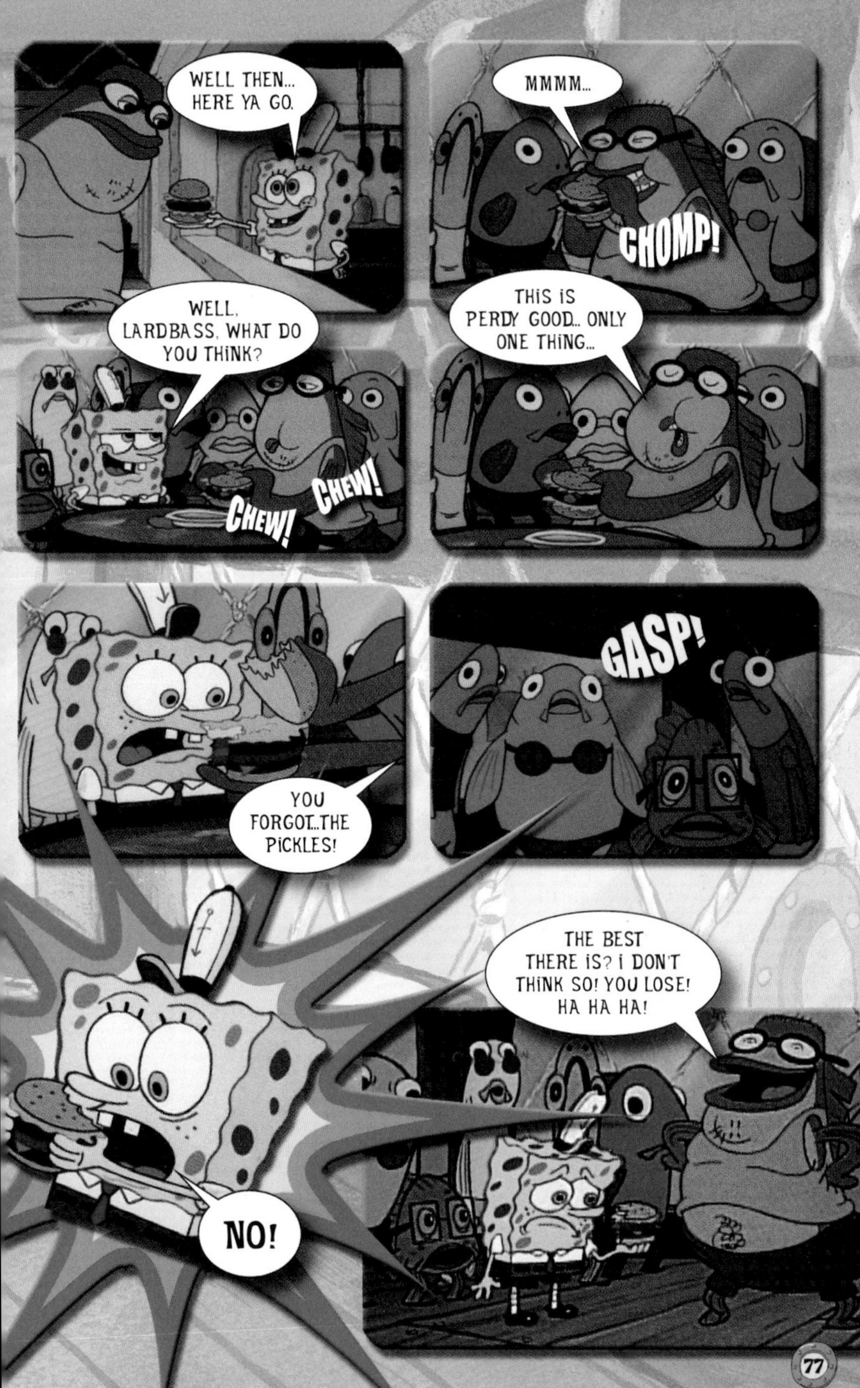

WELL THEN... HERE YA GO.
MMMM...
CHOMP!
WELL, LARDBASS, WHAT DO YOU THINK?
CHEW!
CHEW!
THIS IS PERDY GOOD... ONLY ONE THING...
YOU FORGOT...THE PICKLES!
GASP!
THE BEST THERE IS? I DON'T THINK SO! YOU LOSE! HA HA HA!
NO!

BUT THE PICKLES SHOULD BE RIGHT WHERE THEY ALWAYS ARE! I KNOW I PUT THEM ON! WHERE ARE THOSE PICKLES?
WHERE...?
PICKLES, PICKLES, PICKLES...
GLOOP!
GLOOP!
I BELIEVE YOU OWE ME TWO BUCKS.
TWO BUCKS?
YOUR GUARANTEE...
GALLEY GRUB
KRABBY PATTY..... 2.00
KRUSTY COMBO.... 3.99
KRUSTY DELUXE.... 3.00
~money-back guarantee~

OH, THAT. WELL, CAN'T WE TALK ABOUT THIS?!
'FRAID NOT.
HOW 'BOUT A DISCOUNT ON THE RESTROOM TOKENS? HOW'S ABOUT A FREE GLASS OF WATER? A DOZEN FREE GLASSES OF WATER! I'LL EVEN PUT ICE IN IT!
SOB!
SOB!
NO! COME BACK! TWO DOLLARS! TWO DOLLARS, NOOO...
MR. KRABS, I KNOW I PUT PICKLES ON THAT KRABBY PATTY.
THAT TWO BUCKS IS COMING OUT OF YOUR PAYCHECK.
GET BACK TO WORK! WE GOT ORDERS WAITING.
I NEED A KRABBY PATTY.

OKAY, I'M NOT GONNA BLOW IT THIS TIME!
GLOOP!
LET'S SEE, BUN DOWN, THEN KETCHUP, THEN MUSTARD, THEN...PICKLES? NO...THAT'S NOT RIGHT!
SPLAT!
BUN DOWN, MUSTARD, THEN KETCHUP, LETTUCE, THEN THE PICKLES? NO...MUSTARD DOWN...BUN UP... WHERE'S THE PATTY GO?
PICKLES... KETCHUP... WAIT... SPONGE—THINK! THINK! I'M LOSIN' IT!!!
BUN DOWN— SHOE— MUSTARD—PAN, BUN. NO!!
MR. KRABS, I'M SO CONFUSED I CAN'T REMEMBER HOW TO DO ANYTHING!
WHY DON'T YOU TAKE THE REST OF THE DAY OFF?
OH NO, MR. KRABS! WHO'LL MAKE THE KRABBY PATTIES?!

DON'T WORRY ABOUT THAT. WE GOT SQUIDWARD.
MR. KRABS IS RIGHT. I NEED TO GET MY HEAD STRAIGHT. WAS IT BUN, PATTY, KETCHUP—
GASP!
POINT! POINT!
OF COURSE...HEH HEH.

NO! NO! WAS IT BUN, PATTY, BUN? LESSEE... WAS IT TOMATO, PICKLE, BUN?
BUN, BUN, PATTY
BUN, PATTY, BUN
TOMATO, PICKLE, BUN
NOOO! BUN? BUN? NO, SHOE? ARGH! I'M SO CONFUSED!!!!!!
MAYBE A GOOD NIGHT'S SLEEP WILL HELP ME GET MY HEAD STRAIGHT. WAS IT MATTRESS, MATTRESS, SHEETS, PILLOW, THEN SPONGEBOB? OR...
OH, YEAH, IT WAS MATTRESS... SPONGEBOB, MATTRESS... YEAH... THEN SHEETS, PILLOW!!!
OH, THINK... SPONGE!
AW... THIS ISN'T RIGHT...
G'NIGHT, GARY!

TICK-TOCK
TICK-TOCK
WAIT, THIS ISN'T RIGHT, EITHER... NOPE... UH-UH... NEGATIVE.
COME ON! COME ON! GET IT RIGHT! WRONG. WRONG! WRONG! NOPE! NEGATORY! NYET!
HOOONK!
AND I ALMOST HAD IT!
HOOONK!
ALARM CLOCK—HOW DO I TURN THIS THING OFF? GARY!
HOOONK!
GARY!
HOOONK!

THE KRUSTY KRAB
PATTIES ARE DONE!!
HMMM...
HEY, HE BURNT MY KRABBY PATTY.
HE BURNT MY SHAKE.
YEAH, HE STINKS.
NO! NO! COME BACK...! NO! NO!
ARRRGH!!! I GOTTA GET SPONGEBOB BACK.

SPONGEBOB?!
SPONGEBOB!
MR. KRABS, HELLO. DO YOU HOW DO?
WHY YOU TALKING FUNNY, LAD?
85

i ANYTHING—
CAN'T DO RIGHT
SINCE—BECAUSE
PICKLES.
NONSENSE.
YOU'LL BE BACK
MAKING KRABBY
PATTIES LIKE YOUR
OLD SELF IN NO
TIME.
i THINK
DON'T READY
TO GO BACK TO
WORK, MR.
KRABS.
ALL
WE NEED TO
DO IS GET YOUR
CONFIDENCE BACK. SO
YOU CAN MAKE ME MORE
MONEY...i MEAN,
PATTIES.
i HOW
DO THAT?
IT'S
LIKE RIDING A
BIKE—YOU NEVER
FORGET.

I'M
GONNA HELP
YOU.
MR.
KRABS,
I DON'T KNOW
IF I...
TAKE YOUR
TIME.
NO,
NO, NO...
HMMMMM.

I GOT IT. I GOT IT. IT'S ALL VERY CLEAR TO ME NOW, MR. KRABS.
IT IS?
YES! I FINALLY REALIZED THAT I CAN'T DO IT!! I CAN'T DO IT, MR. KRABS! I'M A FAILURE!!!
DON'T TALK LIKE THAT...
DON'T YA GET IT, YOU CRUSTACEOUS CHEAPSKATE? I CAN'T MAKE A DOUBLE KRABBY PATTY WITH THE WORKS!
I CAN'T PUT A PATTY ON A BUN—WITH LETTUCE, CHEESE, ONIONS, TOMATOES, KETCHUP, MUSTARD, PICKLES AND TOP BUN! TOGETHER IN THAT ORDER!
IT'S TIME...

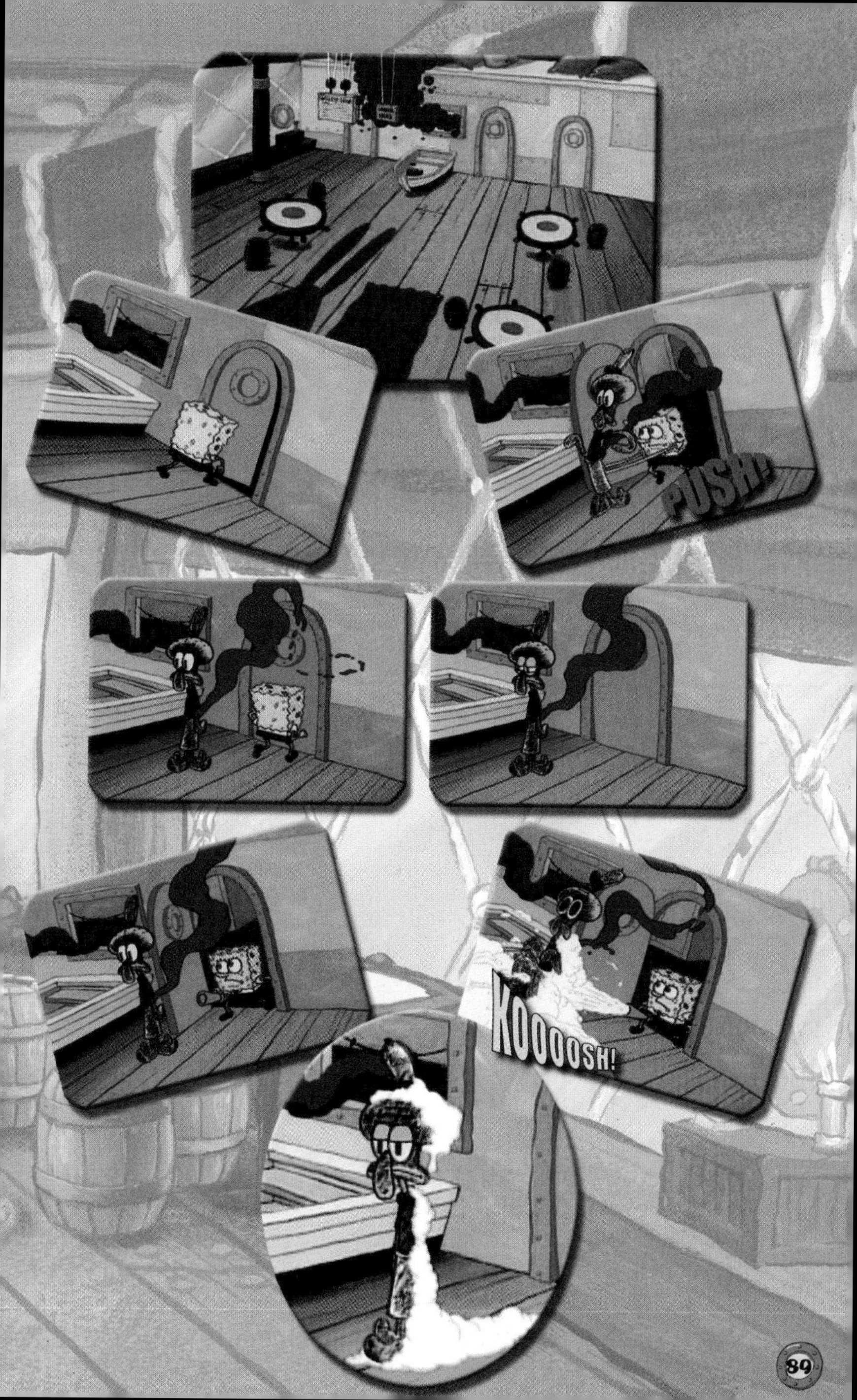
PUSH!
KOOOOSH!

HEY, SPONGEBOB'S BACK!

SPONGEBOB!

HEY!
SPONGEBOB!
HE'S BACK! LOOK!

I HEAR SQUAREPANTS IS BACK.

I'M RIGHT HERE, BUBBLEBASS.

I THOUGHT I RAN YOU OUT OF TOWN.

PA-TOO!

THIS IS WHERE I BELONG.
BLOOP!
GIVE ME THE REGULAR, AND THIS TIME DON'T FORGET THE PICKLES!
I DIDN'T!
CHOMP!
UUHHH?
CHEW!
CHEW!
CHEW!

STILL NO PICKLES!
GASP!
SEE!
YOU FAILED AGAIN, SPONGEBOB LOSERPANTS!
HA!
HA!
HA!
HA!
WAIT A MINUTE.
LOOK! HE'S BEEN HIDING THE PICKLES UNDER HIS TONGUE THE WHOLE TIME!
AND THERE'S THE PICKLES FROM LAST TIME, TOO!

AND THERE'S MY CAR KEYS!
...AND THERE'S MY RIDE!
THREE CHEERS FOR THE RETURN OF OUR MASTER FRY COOK, SPONGEBOB!
HIP-HIP HOORAY! HIP-HIP HOORAY! HIP-HIP HOORAY!
BOOOOOO!
THE KRUSTY KRAB
HIP-HIP BOOOOOO! HIP-HIP BOOOOOO!
END

COMING SOON FROM TOKYOPOP®